THE

LANGUAGE

—— OF ——

INFLUENCE

500
INSIGHTS
FOR LIFE
& LEADING

SCOTT HAGAN

On a good day, enjoy yourself;
On a bad day, examine your conscience.
God arranges for both kinds of days
So that we won't take anything for granted.

Ecclesiastes 7:14

This book is dedicated
to three wonderful friends
who reached inside and pulled
this book out of me.

I'M FOREVER THANKFUL TO:

Gary Zelesky

Michelle Karns (now deceased)

Kwame Anku

I'm also deeply appreciative for the editing
brilliance of my friend Jason Yarbrough.

I also want to thank my friend Andrew Mason
for his input and encouragement,
it was invaluable.

TABLE OF CONTENTS

THIS BOOK IS CONSIDERED AN

an·thol·o·gy

An **an·thol·o·gy** is a published collection of short writings. The Language of Influence is not laid out in traditional book form by chapter titles, but is organized around 500 entries on life and leading.

These entries are for personal reflection or team discussions on influence and leadership.

I believe there's enough material in this book to last you and your team a lifetime.

Enjoy.

PREFACE

The Language of Influence is a collection of original sayings.

I've had fun over the last several years developing these phrases as part of my public presentations on leadership. To date, I've published over 1,500 leadership sayings on social media. This past year, I thought it was time to take the top 500 posts with the most "likes" and "comments" and organize them into a book for leaders and teams. Below I've included several suggestions on ways this book can help organizations of any size become better at what they do.

This book actually began by accident after an innocent Facebook post in 2013. After a friend of mine heard me speak, he asked if he could use some of what I said for a meeting he was leading the next day. I said, "Absolutely, all yours." Later that day he sent me a text. He was trying to remember a phrase I had used and asked if I remembered exactly what I said. To be honest, I vaguely remembered the sentence myself, but came up with this: "Great leaders pay attention, poor leaders seek attention." He quickly texted back, "That's it!"

His reaction gave me the idea to post that one-liner on my personal Facebook wall. It quickly lit up with 'likes' and sparked a flurry of conversation. My selfies and puppy pictures never got that kind of reaction, so maybe people were more interested in some free social media leadership content than I thought. So, for fun, I posted another leadership saying the next day and the reaction was similar. After a few weeks, my close friend, Kwame Anku, told me I needed to launch a dedicated Facebook page just for these leadership sayings. So, with a little urging from Kwame, my hastily named "Note2Leaders" Facebook page was born on March 19, 2013.

Over the past 3 years the page has grown to over 100,000 followers, including some 30,000 young English-speaking professionals from the Middle East. Apparently, the hunger to grow as a leader is global. I'm learning that people, no matter their age, want to grow their influence the right way. After seeing the response to the "Note2Leaders" Facebook page, it's clear to me that people want to be virtue-based influencers.

This material has been presented all over the world. I've shared it with professional and college coaches and athletes, politicians, business champions, prison wardens and even members of the U.S. Special Forces. Everyone always agrees: this material changed their ability to influence!

Hopefully, it will have the same influence on you.

HOW TO GET THE MOST OUT OF THIS BOOK

WEEKLY TEAM EXERCISE

The recommended size for this exercise is 4 to 15 people.

Have a different team member lead the discussion each week by following the template below. Let the rotation continue until each person has had a turn (ex: If you have 4 team members, do this exercise for four weeks; 8 team members goes for 8 weeks).

- Choose one of the statements that stood out to you and read it to the group.

- Give a brief explanation of why it stood out and how it spoke to you.

Handpick 3–5 of the questions from the list below and present them to the team for group discussion:

1. How does this speak to you when you hear it?

2. Can you think of a leader or person who has embodied this maxim in their life?

3. Is this principle counter-intuitive to your instincts, emotions and/or patterns of thinking? If yes, explain.

4. What are the potential negative consequences of neglecting or ignoring this statement?

5. In your area(s) of responsibility, how can living out this concept improve your influence and effectiveness?

6. How would our team benefit if all of us modeled this value as we worked together?

THE 2 DOORS...

The most beautiful thing in life is opportunity.

When the desire to do something meets the
possibility for it to happen, the human heart comes alive.

Opportunity, however, usually presents itself through
two vastly different doors. You look through the first
door and say, "I can make this opportunity great."

Why?

Because you already possess what it takes
to succeed on the other side. In other words,
the opportunity needs you.

But when you look through the second door,
you see something far different. You see a
much greater risk and say to yourself,
"I must *become* great in order to succeed."

Always choose the second door.

Through the first door you bring who you
already are, but through the second door,
you bring the potential of what you must become.

There are two types of leaders. Those who love power and those who love people.

You cannot hide your heart. Whatever fills, spills.

The attitude is always louder than the answer.

Criticizing someone is how the underachiever compliments himself.

Think twice about severing
a valued relationship
because a piece of you will
be leaving with them.

We imitate who
we admire. So be careful
who you admire.

Discovering something
new is good.
Rediscovering something
lost is better.

Arrogance is worse than ignorance.

The mission of a leader is to make complex things simple; it's never to make simple things complex.

Great leaders
pay attention.
Poor leaders
seek attention.

A big part of
leadership is
knowing when
to shut up.

Coming across as the smartest person in the room is highly overrated.

When you
serve others,
the bitterness
from not
being served
is washed
away.

Even if you were born
for something, you still
have to learn how to do it.

Being lied to is worse
than being lied about.

The purpose for
memories is to keep
you grateful.

A good reputation is based on two things: keeping your promises and keeping your cool.

018

Help people
live up to their
potential, not your
expectations.

019

A leader must
produce more
than they
consume.

Momentum doesn't require something monumental. Approach your next inch with passion and you'll be fine.

Value them first, evaluate second.

There is no such thing as trying to be honest.

Sometimes all you can do to stop the chaos is build a greenhouse and grow something new.

Rarely is the wind at your back at precisely the moment you need it. It's usually in your face making you stronger.

Even if it lasts a lifetime, it's still temporary.

Success is not about second chances. It's about second choices.

027

When you grow,
they grow.

028

Fast humility
cleans up a lot
of messes.

Not being chosen is only a crisis if you make it one.

It's not about your resume. It's about your relationships.

The fastest way to taste
the contents of your heart
is to hear your enemy
complimented.

It takes someone
ten years to forget
you lied to them.

The mouth reveals
the heart.

You cannot inspire
people to live outside
the box when you
personally lead from
inside the circle.

Going first is
entirely different
than being first.

A true leader never
stops on a negative.

It's never about your passion alone. It's far more about your capacity to draw out unscripted passion in others.

The anxiety leading up to the confrontation is always worse than the actual confrontation.

Taking responsibility is different than simply saying you're sorry.

A grudge will never lead to justice.

041

What marks a great leader is not their inability to offend, but their inability to be offended.

042

I applaud those who build bridges. I stop applauding if they add a toll booth.

043

It's impossible to build a team if nobody enjoys being around you.

Nothing is more
rewarding than
doing something
great for someone
and having it go
completely unnoticed.

Accountability is
what gives you the
confidence to
stand alone.

Never follow a
leader who
isn't following
a leader.

Anything done
with sincerity
has the power
to grow.

Listening is
entirely different
than not talking.

Managing distractions is the one skill set that separates the average leader from the excellent leader.

Success requires
self-denial
instead of
self-promotion.

You do not move
the unstructured
toward structure.
You move the
unstructured
toward trust.

052

People want
to be mentored,
not monitored.

053

Being bold only
works if what
you're saying
is true.

054

Little gestures
move big
mountains.

It takes
rest to run.
It's impossible
for an
exhausted
leader to stay
motivated.

A wrong
hire is
subtraction
by addition.

No matter how
mundane
it gets, stay
relentless
about your
family.

Twenty years
goes by
very quickly
when you're
a leader.

Stop living
suspicious.
Start smiling
at people you
don't know.

The irony of masks is that we wear them to appear strong, yet people are drawn to us when we take them off.

Leadership is a mix of iron and water. One part is unbending; the other part is fluid and adaptive.

Keep the vision adventurous but the relationships safe.

Don't let a new friend take the place of an old friend. Have two friends.

The secret to high capacity leadership is knowing how to turn personal criticism into personal improvement.

065

Nothing
improves on
its own.

066

The secret to longevity
is simple: don't self-
destruct.

067

Insecurity will
emotionally rearrange
everything you see
and hear as a leader.

A big part of leadership
is making complete
strangers feel at ease.

The status quo
cannot defeat
the status quo.

Leadership is about
helping people take
steady steps before
quantum leaps.

Never hide your sources. When you talk about the role others have played in your success, people instinctively know you can be trusted.

Don't worry about the credit. People will never forget who inspired them.

A wise leader can see the bad inside the good and the good inside the bad.

Good looks is not where God looks. His criteria is the heart.

Being missed is better than being noticed.

Procrastination doubles the price of everything.

The example is the expert.

Leadership is not about turning something small into something big. It's about turning something lonely into something loved.

079

Leadership happens personally before it happens professionally.

080

Building a new relationship is good; restoring a broken one is even better.

081

Align yourself with a team that is talent rich but ego poor. If you can't find one, then form one.

Put success on the
bottom shelf so
anyone can reach it.

Whether physical
or emotional, you
have to cleanse the
wound before you
close the wound.
Infection is deadly.

It's not whether you're outstanding today, but whether you're still standing tomorrow.

I would rather
be naive
than
calloused.

Focus on
living —
not reliving.

If you need guarantees, you cannot lead.

Maturity is about doing less, not more.

Leadership happens
over time, not overnight.

Asking questions to
discover the truth
is different than
questioning something
that is already true.

Giving up on someone
becomes your loss,
not theirs.

092

People notice reactions more than actions.

093

It's not what you plant. It's what you cultivate.

No matter how tired, scattered or frustrated you become, a great leader is always in control of what comes out of their mouths.

Talking is good.
Just pick a different
topic than yourself.

The four most important
words in leadership are
"LET THERE BE LIGHT".

You know you're doing
life right when you don't
have a difficult time
falling asleep at night.

Don't confuse
your role with
your potential.

Whatever you've gone
through is to help those
now going through.

Honesty speeds
up the solution.

101

Be persuasive.
Just don't lie
while doing it.

102

A smart leader
sees potential
in the outcast.

103

Most conflict
happens when an
under-reaction collides
with an over-reaction.

Offering a
timid hint is
not leadership.
People want
their leader
to speak
with courage
and clarity.

Every time
you tell a lie,
even casually,
a piece of your
conscience dies.

It's about the
individual, not
the audience.

Make friends with reality
as fast as you can.

Focus on wisdom and
better decision-making
will naturally follow.

Standing alone is
entirely different
than being alone.

People reinvest in bad decisions because of pride. It's far better to let humility set you free.

Never insult suffering by confusing it with inconvenience.

The worst scenario for any organization is having an insecure leader holding power and making decisions.

The only way to keep fear from ruling your life is to first keep it from ruling your day.

You will never achieve excellence by living just one notch above the lowest common denominator.

You cannot threaten people into loyalty.

Nothing has a shorter life span than applause.

Being
passionate and
entrepreneurial
without
good family
habits will
take you
nowhere.

Behavior does not
affect love, but it
does affect trust.

Every time you brag
about yourself,
you become less
noticeable.

Listen to the person
instead of trying to
read their mind.

Your neighbor
is the person
next to you
at any given
moment.

Unless you believe
in the principle,
you cannot
endure the
process.

Faith moves
the mountains
before you.
Humility
moves the
mountains
inside of you.

No organization has ever thrived under the leadership of a control freak.

Your behaviors are your brand.

Destiny is never instant; that's why good leaders give things time to grow.

An effective leader never dismisses people or opportunities after one glance.

The worst
kind of
selfishness
is self-pity.
It takes the
energy out
of everyone
in the room.

Your intuition reports
to your core values.

129

It takes an enormous
amount of energy to live
your life avoiding people.

130

Your most important
mental skill is the
ability to think twice.

131

There's nothing
wrong with
being invisible
and laying
low. It's good
medicine for your
leadership soul.

Leadership is a combination of your motor and your motive. It takes an equal mix of energy and expertise to become great at what you do.

An effective leader
knows the difference
between a symptom
and a cause.

Betrayal, though a
terrible wound, has
the power to transform
your life for the good
of many. Betrayal is
often the pathway
to promotion.

Occasionally
people need
their leaders to
be poetic and
inspirational.
Most of the time
they need them
to be pointed
and practical.

Never try to guide or decide something until after your emotions are rejuvenated.

Solitude is a gift, not a punishment.

Real change means you become new, not just different. It involves new actions, new ambitions, new attitudes and new investments.

140

Leadership is a tough calling. It requires coping with uncertainty, boredom, isolation, negativity, and, on rare occasions, success.

141

Worship God.
Love people.
Manage things.

A child is born to love, not to hate.

The talent of a great leader isn't their talent. It's their ability to spot talent and collide with it.

Discernment is not the ability to know right from wrong. It's the ability to know right from almost right.

Leadership is about solutions, not ceremonies.

If you gave the gift in hopes of earning their love, you gave the gift in vain.

The only thing a leader can impart to a protégé is their burden. Gifting comes from above.

Never demean
someone's sincere
attempt at
something.

Two things mark a
great organization:
clarity and charity.

People do not respect you because you've done something great. They respect you because you've done something right.

Anxiety is self-inflicted.

Being wise is better than being right.

Improvement
is more
satisfying
than
achievement.

Think twice —
speak once.

You don't have to be ridiculously gifted. You just have to be ridiculously committed.

People connect
with your
struggle
before they
connect
with your
success.

Self-pity
destroys
a team. It
reduces the
well-being of
the whole to
the well-being
of the one.

Your job is to help
them up, not straighten
them up.

It's not what you achieve.
It's what you set in motion.

A clock and a calendar
cannot organize a
man's heart.

Being your best is entirely different than trying to be better than someone else.

Don't destroy your competitor for the sake of gain. Do the exact opposite: serve and resource them.

Don't believe the cynic.
People are still moved
by virtue.

Secrecy is different
than confidentiality.

Be wary of anything that
is perfectly organized
and totally successful.

The most relevant thing a leader can do is be predictable.

Study makes you fluent. Purity makes you potent.

People will
never follow
someone
they fear.

The extra mile
is where the
treasure lies.

Hard things make us choose between growth and bitterness. There's no third choice.

Revenge actively destroys. Grudge bearing passively destroys.

An average
leader
Tolerates.

A good leader
Celebrates.

A great leader
Elevates.

Comeback
stories and
second chances
still move the
human heart
more than
anything else.

174

Most solutions aren't obvious; that's why it requires a leader.

175

A leader helps people stay enthusiastic about the right things.

176

The encourager is always the most memorable person in the room.

Adversity is rarely about the difficult task. It's usually about the difficult people.

Gifted leaders do more than confront people. What they do is draw them out of the shadows so they can confront themselves.

The best way to
stop thinking about
something is
to stop talking
about it.

I've never once
looked at a
person who
asked for advice
as weak.

Dreaming
is part of
leadership —
wishing
is not.

Confidence
is instilled,
not inherited.

The best
organizations
are more fluid
than rigid.

No matter how
a child starts in
life, the presence
of an inspiring
mentor can change
everything.

Confidence
is different
than courage.
Confidence helps
you stand while
courage helps
you stand alone.

Seek help.
Never seek pity.

Good leaders
follow-up.
Great leaders
follow through.

Organization is good but mobilization is better.

Leadership is not a competition.

Spreading division
usually starts
by spreading
dissatisfaction.

An effective
leader knows the
difference between
policy and love.

192

Be thankful before
it arrives, not after.

193

Failure is
refining, not
defining.

194

Always conclude
with hope,
even after a
confrontation.

"I taught you" is different than "I told you".

Average leaders rise against. Great leaders rise above.

Speak from experience, not tradition.

A flow chart is
not a vision.

Make the decision
with them, not
for them.

Every leader of
substance has at least
one story of betrayal
along the way.

Influence is different
than popularity.

Your humility is
more important
than your gift.

Being thoughtful is
more important than
being vocal.

204

I would rather
be an advocate
than an adversary.

205

Transparency is the
shortest path to
deliverance.

206

One of the
greatest privileges
in life is to help
alleviate suffering.

People want to follow a vision that is organic, not orchestrated.

The reality of leadership is that you spend as much time pulling weeds as you do planting flowers.

Never chase respect. Live an honorable life and respect will find you.

If you're not feeding them, you're not leading them.

Overreaction is not leadership.

Toxic leaders put their own needs first. Proceed with caution.

Being a visionary is
good, but a leader needs
to be more of a doer
than a dreamer.

Confidence has more
stamina than enthusiasm.

A leader's heart must
stay hot. Once it becomes
room temperature,
influence ceases.

Whatever
you neglect
deteriorates.

Most things
never start
growing until
after they are
broken.

Never punish
the next person
because of
the actions of
the pervious
person. Each
relationship is
a clean slate.

At the heart of all
leadership is teaching.

Excess is not success.
True leaders live
more moderate than
privileged.

Slay your distractions,
don't try to
manage them.

222

Self-pity is not humility.

223

People may obey rigid leadership, but they will not follow it.

224

Leadership is filled with moods and moving parts, so just focus on the mission and stay genuine.

A root is
different than
a result.

It takes
tremendous
courage to not
admit you
were right.

The absence of
integrity keeps
a gifted person
from becoming an
influential leader.

Burnout is the result
of anxiety not fatigue.
You overcome burnout
by worrying less,
not working less.

Love is not a livelihood. 99% of the people you help in life will never be able to compensate you for it.

Rejection is what they do to me. Dejection is what I do to myself.

People without hope don't need a speech. They need hope.

Successful leaders have two characteristics. They're well-grounded and well-surrounded.

Leadership is totally different than management. A manager makes sure it's functioning, while a leader makes certain it's reaching its potential.

People need
leaders
who are
responsive,
not defensive.

When I compare
myself to
someone else,
I always lose
my way.

Nothing is more dangerous than a highly-motivated person with wrong motives.

It's impossible to help someone grow when they interpret "correction" as "rejection".

Leadership requires both attention span and willpower.

In leadership, your private life matters more than your public life.

You cannot
force people
to stop feeling
something.
You can only
help them
start to feel
something
new.

241

The leader is the one who loves more, not the one who knows more.

242

The test comes now; the reason why comes later. It's called the law of learning.

243

Ethics cannot be woven in at a later date; it must be the original thread.

A relationship
is better than
a profit.

Never collect your
compliments.
Toss them to the
next person as
fast as you can.

Just because you disagree with someone doesn't mean their actions should offend you.

Make sure you know the whole story before making someone your hero.

The only distraction
that matters is
your family.

It's always about
their achievements,
not yours.

When it comes to
ending a feud,
somebody has
to go first.

What separates
one leader from the
next is their ability
to notice things.

Coping with
uncertainty is much
easier when there's
an encouraging
friend nearby.

Whatever you
can't talk about,
owns you.

253

The cowardly
will always
resent the brave.

254

The first goal
of leadership is
to set standards,
not goals.

255

Be hot or cold.
Never be passive.

You can fake
breadth, but you
can't fake depth.

The problem with
a bad foundation
is that it can take
years to discover it.

There is a big difference between a genuine problem and an imagined one.

The quality of your life is determined by how you spend your time and with whom you spend it.

Being decisive
is different than
being aggressive.
Aggression is
counterfeit authority.

CONSISTENCY
means we are
experiencing a
repetition of
results.

EXECUTION
means we are performing as planned.

EXCELLENCE
means we are doing it the right way every time.

EFFORT means we
are staying strong
through the struggle.

Great leaders notice the
positive before they
notice the negative.

Your heart follows
your money;
most people think
it's the other
way around.

A savvy
leader can
spot the clues.

Always keep
your heart twice
the size of
your brain.

Everything starts with effort; the momentum comes later.

Being profound usually happens by accident.

Generosity is different than giving.

The best thing about having close friends is that they can tell when you're faking it.

The best leaders tend to be more cooperative than competitive.

I'll take an average idea in the hands of a great leader over a great idea in the hands of an average leader any day.

Trying hard to impress people usually leaves a bad impression.

One of the most difficult places in leadership is the space between faithfulness and fruitfulness.

The hardest part of leadership is correcting someone you love. It's much easier to correct a stranger.

Leadership is not about making the hard decision. It's about making the wise decision.

The greatest gift in life is to be free of your secrets.

Emotionally healthy leaders practice two things well: gratitude for the past and excitement for the future.

It doesn't matter if the crowd laughs or applauds, all that matters is whether or not they trust you.

Your destiny is about
your decisions,
not your talents.

Creativity is the icing,
not the cake.

A leader can't speak a
clear message when they
are carrying a contradiction
in their heart.

Successful
leaders know that
credible always
comes before
incredible.

If it requires
lying, don't
do it.

Even smart
people need
time to process
change.
Don't rush
through
important
decisions.

A good leader
makes you aware;
a great leader
makes you
anticipate.

Being secretive
is different than
being private.

Dream big
and share the
vision, but don't
exaggerate.
People will not
follow someone
who lies.

It's not healthy
to fret over
people's opinions
of you.

Just encourage
them to grow.
Don't try to
make them into
something else.

294

Words do not wash off
the soul like highway
graffiti. Words are
rarely neutral; they
either heal or wound.

295

It's about the cause,
not the applause.

296

Growing leaders
create growing
things.

A good leader will assess the problem and determine if the change needs to be sweeping or surgical. Very few situations are exactly the same.

If it's getting
tougher,
it means
you're getting
stronger.

No resolve,
no results.

299

300

Power is not
the prize.

301

Never follow a leader who refuses to admit they were wrong.

302

Now is better than later.

Don't brush aside the person who has been to hell and back. You want them on your team. They have now become the person everyone hoped they would.

304

The title comes later,
not first.

305

The easy reaction is to
retaliate. It takes real
leadership to restore,
reconcile and rebuild.

306

Not every person who
fails is a fake. Good
people makes mistakes,
even big ones.

No one has
the energy or
expertise to be
the catalyst on
every project.
Sometimes
your role is to
support another
person's idea.

Some birth, some build, some bless. You will be invited to do all three dimensions during your leadership life.

Things do not compete for your time. They compete for your affections.

It's not enough to thank people publicly. You also need to thank them personally and privately.

Your countenance is a message all its own.

Never feel badly for helping someone remember their promises. You're actually helping them remain whole.

The right outcome
requires the right outlook.

It's not whether or not it
makes sense to you. It's
whether or nor it makes
sense to them.

Boasting makes you
less noticeable.

A dialogue is better than an explanation.

It has to happen to me before it can happen through me.

The best way to distinguish yourself is by including others.

A small step is
still progress.

319

It's more important
to be truthful
than talented.

320

The best defense
is to not
be defensive.

321

It takes courage to tell a young leader that you see their gaps, not just their gifts, and that you are equally committed to both.

Creativity is critical, but not as critical as the message.

The difference between the bitter and the bittersweet is whether or not you have learned something through the process.

You cannot love a cause; you can only love people.

Being bored is more dangerous than being tired. Your greatest protection is purpose.

Your reputation
will always
be there to
greet you.

Nothing is more
contagious than
confidence.

You cannot lead with equity and fairness if you still have suspicions about the people you've never met.

Truth always prevails.
{Joe Elston}

330

331

Showing interest in
someone is not enough;
you have to invest in
their life.

332

It's tough to lead when
you're in a bad mood.

333

Patience is not the enemy of passion.

334

The easy road will not get you there.

335

The art of teamwork is in knowing how to sharpen the countenance of your teammates.

Just as many people misunderstand a visionary as understand them.

Leadership is about helping people move from dysfunction to well-being.

Don't sell, demonstrate.

If you think for too long about a missed opportunity, chances are you'll miss the next one too.

An image will never conquer a reputation.

The richest person
on earth is the one
who gives the most
mercy away.

Empowering is better
than delegating.

It's about standing
on something, not
reaching for something.

Denial is not optimism.

You can't fake sincerity.

Nothing significant is ever accomplished after one attempt.

Nothing is more disheartening than to invest in someone who lacks motivation.

348

The average person
is above average.

349

Never trust a
leader who wants
to be famous.

350

Successful people
have a passion for
the process, not just
the results.

Nothing is a finished product. Everything is a work in progress.

You cannot control people, but you can guide, counsel and inspire them.

A great leader stands firmly on a foundation, not a pedestal.

The ability to stand alone comes from knowing you are never alone. God is always with you.

People feel empowered by your example, not your instruction.

Some of the best learning happens when there's no place to hide.

There are four delivery systems for learning: conscience, counsel, correction and calamity. Pay attention early in the process.

358

Faking an answer is
a sign of insecurity,
not confidence.

359

No matter how
much you disagree,
you must still treat
that person
with dignity.

Make sure you are threatening the status quo, not the people.

Skills are entirely different than talents.

Even the best version of you still has flaws.

To get clean, you
have to come clean.

363

A manager makes
people behave.
A leader makes
people believe.

364

If it comes too easily
it will probably
be forgotten.

365

An effective leader gives people both permission and perspective.

A great leader doesn't run from high expectations.

Trying to handle
pressure all
by yourself
produces only
one outcome:
debilitating
stress.

369

It's impossible to be
fruitful without first
being faithful.

370

Happiness and
productivity go
hand in hand.

371

In the end, it's the
desire not the dream
that brings results.

Know your audience, not just your material.

372

Favor is entirely different than fame.

373

Being right is not the same as being wise.

374

375

Leading the charge is different than being in charge.

376

Help people live up to their potential, not your expectations.

377

Stop fighting with the ones you love — life is too brief.

You have to
see the goal,
not just set
the goal.

Focus on your
relationships,
not your rights.

People do not change because of an open mind; they change because of an open heart.

The greatest enemy to human achievement is human nature.

The best leaders are those who have a good relationship between their mind and their mouth.

Nothing of meaning ever goes uncontested.

If you can listen to feedback without getting defensive, it will ignite a growth culture throughout your entire organization.

Regret is not the road to something worse; it's a nasty destination all its own.

Living in the moment is good; staying in the moment is not.

A healthy leader
doesn't hide his
emotions,
but he does
manage them.

The fastest way to
bring your team
culture back from
the dead is to flood
it with genuine
appreciation.

A leader can feel
the absence of
something, not
just the presence
of something.

Your success does
not steal my potential.
There's plenty of
wind in the harbor
for more than one
ship to sail.

People want their leader consistently good, not inconsistently great.

Average leaders make an impact. Great leaders reproduce.

No matter what type of organization you lead, doctrine comes before vision. What you believe together is more important than what you see together.

No matter how strong your leadership gift, you cannot lead a disinterested person.

Casual lying is how professional liars practice.

A big part of leadership is knowing how to make complete strangers feel at ease.

It's easy to listen to flattery because it leaves all the exaggeration up to someone else.

You don't wait for things to calm down before saying you're sorry; you say you're sorry to help things calm down.

The split second you
ask for help, all past
perceptions of your
arrogance vanishes,
the effect is that
powerful.

When you minimize
another person's
achievements,
you are the one
who shrinks.

Saying nothing
when a compliment
is needed is
worse than being
derogatory.

Being angry is
different than
being hurt.

People will never
forget the person
who made them
feel stupid
in public.

I've never met
a person who is
both critical and
generous.

What makes your organization soar are the stories, not the stats.

Panic breeds panic, so remain calm through the chaos.

People get weary
of following
a leader who
talks big but
never follows
through.

Leadership is
about instilling
bravery
and buy-in.

Worry is about tomorrow. Anxiety is about today. One attacks the mind, the other the stomach. Both are out to defeat your leadership.

There are two types of leaders in life. Those running toward something, and those running from something.

God gave us relationships to replenish us, not diminish us.

Most people are overwhelmed by debt and regret; the joy of leadership is to help them feel optimistic again.

413

Being a leader should
bring out the best in you,
not the worst in you.

414

Being honest with a
friend is not an act
of disloyalty.

415

Focus on discovery
instead of being
discovered.

Great leaders
understand you
have to change an
atmosphere before
you can change a
culture.

You cannot turn
back the clock,
but you can
redeem the day.

For an organization to be dynamic, the relationships must create energy, not burn energy.

How do you teach
a young leader to
keep their promise?
By keeping
your own first.

It's not the difficulty
that is difficult;
it's having to face
it alone.

Complacency means you're technically alive but functionally dead.

Leadership is never about stuff and status. It's about service and sacrifice.

A delay means it was probably more important than you originally thought.

Fame extracts; it rarely adds.

Preparing your mind helps you present. Preparing your heart helps you persuade.

Never follow a leader who comes across like a messiah or a martyr.

427

Reconciliation means the relationship has been delivered of revenge and anxiety.

428

A passion for leadership begins with a love for people.

429

Leadership is a lifestyle, not a role.

Integrity means that what you thought, what you said and what you did are all the same.

A healthy leader has two basic traits: they can receive love and they can give love.

There is always someone in the room who feels left out, like a mouse without a hole. Your job is to find them.

Success has two inconvenient demands: getting started and finishing well.

Insecure leaders usually do whatever is necessary to avoid personal feedback.

Nothing distorts team mission like petty jealousy.

The true leader is the one who loves more; it's not the one who knows more.

The best kind of leaders are both daring and caring.

A great team is not
where the proven
leaders perform;
it's where the rising
leaders develop.

Support them, don't
rescue them. Just
encourage them to
listen and learn along
the difficult road.
It's how we grow.

440

Most chaos is temporary.

441

Simplicity is a sign of brilliance.

442

A faithful leader doesn't abandon his people even if he feels abandoned by them.

A good attitude
is better than a
good idea.

Great leaders
turn mistakes
into information.

445

Great leaders notice and praise incremental successes.

446

Great leaders know the difference between patience and procrastination.

447

The only way to see your blind spot is to listen to feedback.

Suffering is a mission.

Survival is never
the goal. Even in
disappointment,
you were born
to influence.

If the idea can be
accomplished by one
person, then it wasn't
a big enough idea.

Focusing on lost opportunities brings regret and defeat. Focusing on future opportunities brings renewal, growth and energy.

452

When something becomes famous, some of the greatness is usually lost.

453

The mountain is moved through great partnerships, not great individuals.

454

Don't just mimic the behaviors of great leaders. Study their behaviors.

455

Focus more on staying motivated and less on being motivational.

456

Technology cannot replace tenacity.

457

One of the most important functions of leadership is intervention, which helps limit the duration of a crisis.

I would rather deal with someone's hidden agenda than with someone's hidden emotions.

Job titles carry very little weight because influence is earned, not assigned.

People become
great because
they're molded
and developed,
not because
of good luck or
good genes.

Peace of mind
is greater
than material
prosperity.

The only way to
erase the affects
of bad leadership
is to inject better
leadership.

Just because someone thinks you're important doesn't mean you have influence.

Most people feel defensive in the presence of arrogance.

A financial secret is just as deadly as a sexual secret.

465

466

Organization is good. Mobilization is better.

Talk about the things you love and you'll never be judged as insincere.

The most important people doing the most important things are largely unknown.

No matter how popular you become, your fate is determined by what you do behind closed doors.

Some people are weathered and dry from reckless living, yet they still have dreams. Don't give up on them.

It's not your resume; it's your relationships.

Every time you put yourself down, you take another step backwards and make the journey longer than it needs to be.

When someone
takes notice of your
potential, it's one
of the best days
of your life.

The challenge is not
your message. The
challenge is whether
or not they receive you
as the messenger.

It's a myth
that if you
hang around
successful
people, you will
automatically
become
successful.

People are drawn to the leader who is in relationship with something stronger than themselves.

A wise leader knows the difference between cooperation and compromise.

A leader must live something, not just say something.

Absorb, reflect,
improve…
it's about
moving on.

Your countenance
means more
to your
career than
you realize.

The greatest gift
a leader gives
his community
is to locate the
abandonment
and remove it.
It's what made
the Samaritan
"Good".

If you lose your cool and scream at people, it will take them five years to forget that experience.

Good leaders make it interesting. Great leaders make it fascinating.

People don't need
a persona. They
need an actual
person who cares
about them.

Never use pity to
get the promotion.
Once people stop
feeling sorry for you,
their interest in
you will end.

Apathy devours
potential. You stop
planning once you
stop caring.

Leadership is
about opening up
your life, not just
your mouth.

Never bind your affections to the traits and tendencies that lie beneath. Bind them to the timeless and true secrets that come down from above.

489

Knowing your season
is good. Knowing your
next step is better.

490

Your problem is not the
problem. Your problem
is not believing
there's a solution.

491

I will take a handful
of friends over a roomful
of spectators any day.

492

Hard is different
than impossible.

493

The recovery time
after an outburst of
anger takes longer
than you think.

494

A wise leader knows
how to be direct
without being
destructive.

There's a difference between having a meeting and feeling a connection.

The only way to become exceptional is to never see yourself as the exception.

Never behave symbolically.

Every decision is a blend of emotions and objectivity.

The moment you admit your mistake, all the necessary components for greatness fall back into place.

Grace has only one first name:

AMAZING.